Reflections for Working Women

Reflections for Working Women

Common Sense, Sage Advice, and Unconventional Wisdom

Carol A. Turkington

McGraw-Hill
New York   San Francisco   Washington, D.C.   Auckland   Bogotá
Caracas   Lisbon   London   Madrid   Mexico City   Milan
Montreal   New Delhi   San Juan   Singapore
Sydney   Tokyo   Toronto

McGraw-Hill

*A Division of The **McGraw·Hill** Companies*

1 2 3 4 5 6 7 8 9 0   DOC/DOC   9 0 1 0 9 8 7 6

ISBN 0-07-065521-9

The sponsoring editor for this book was Susan Barry, the editing supervisor was Pattie Amoroso, and the production supervisor was Donald F. Schmidt. It was set in Palatino by Terry Leaden of McGraw-Hill's Professional Book Group composition unit.

Printed and bound by R. R. Donnelley & Sons Company.

To working women everywhere,
whose only limits are the bars
we place on our own horizon

Contents

Leadership

Techniques

The Day to Day

The Big Picture

Preface

I've been a working woman for 27 years, but what I know about work is *my* truth. There are a lot of other truths, and I wouldn't have been able to write this book without help from scores of other women who generously shared their time, their insights, and their advice via computer on-line services and personal interviews.

"What has been important to you as a working woman?" I asked them. "What do you wish you had known when you started your first job? What is the best advice you would give your own daughter as she starts out in the working world?" I also asked for strategies, suggestions, and tips on coping with the pressures of balancing home and work life.

The reflections within these pages have been culled from questionnaires and interviews with many women from all walks of life: cashiers, waitresses, hairdressers, floral shop owners, physicians, lawyers, teachers, artists, writers, publishers, business executives, secretaries, editors, stable workers, cooks, students, bankers, investment counselors, clerks, psychologists. All the women were eager to share what they learned.

What surprised me were the similar themes running through all the interviews, no matter what job the woman held, how old she was, or what part of the country she lived in. *Have a mentor*, they said. *Make sure you have lots of support*. And time and again, over and over, all women echoed the same refrain: *You can't have it all, do it all, be all things to all people. You must choose your battles and streamline your priorities*. This also means knowing what aspects of your life to let slide.

Interestingly, what some of the most successful of the women report is that their happiness is not measured in what others might term success: a bigger promotion, a better job, a more impressive house. What many of these women express is that the more successful they became, the more they realized their happiness lay in the small, quiet moments: time with their children, their partners, time spent pursuing a beloved hobby or perfecting a neglected talent. In an unpredictable world fraught with downsizing, chauvinism, company politics, and sexism, these women reveal that it is the small, exquisite moments of life that are the most enduring.

It is true that sometimes in my interviews, I encountered anger. I saw resignation. Sometimes I found bitterness. But I also uncovered vast oceans of hope and eddies of quiet strength. I found dignity, humor, compassion, and honesty. There was a real sense among the women to whom I spoke of a shared purpose, of a willingness to help other women avoid the mistakes of those who came before them. Writing this book has bolstered my hopes for the future of all women, whether they choose to work inside or outside the home. What I have learned from my interviews has given me hope for the world of work which my own daughter will someday inherit.

Because there is still much to be done, it is seductively easy to spend our time obsessing about how far we still must go to achieve parity in the world of work, how many more stereotypes there are to be put to rest, how many abuses there are still to correct. There is also value in taking time to reflect how far we have come. If you want to measure that distance, you have to look no farther than the nearest kindergarten. In the world of 5-year-olds, some gender stereotypes still prevail: The little girls all like pink Barbies and the boys all want to play with war toys. But when a little boy told my daughter that girls couldn't be astronauts, she looked at him and snapped, "Don't be silly!" and stalked away.

It was not so long ago that my own mother asked me and my sister why on earth we wanted to "settle for" a career instead of a life as a housewife. It was only 20 years later that my 4-year-old daughter, after being introduced to a male surgeon, asked me incredulously: "Can boys be doctors, too?"

Carol A. Turkington

Far away there in the sunshine
are my highest aspirations.
I may not reach them,
but I can look up
and see their beauty,
believe in them,
and try to follow where they lead.
— Louisa May Alcott

Reflections
for
Working
Women

At Home

DON'T DEAL WITH WORK AT HOME

Sensible solutions to problems at work don't depend on worrying about them endlessly in your spare time.

In More Depth

The higher your stress level, the less effective you'll be on the job—so don't bring your work home with you. You need some time off in order to recharge your batteries. Try to compartmentalize your work stress so you don't allow the pressures of the job to interfere with your leisure time.

Make sure you have some enjoyable things to do in your spare time, so that you are occupied with fun, stress-relieving activities. Some fairly driven women make the mistake of being just as driven about their play as they are about work. The key here is to *relax*. Exercise can help relieve stress, but only if it is never a source of guilt. Otherwise, what's the point?

The Idea in Action

Lauren is a secretary for a small but hectic law firm. When the partners realized how talented she was, they began piling on more and more work. Perfectionistic to the point of compulsion, Lauren began taking files home to work on them at night. She spent endless hours worrying about filing systems and ways to streamline the office. Whenever any of the partners asked her to stay late to help with a project, she was always available. All she could talk about at home were the partners, their cases, and petty problems in the office. It was not until her husband objected to her complete absorption in her work that she realized the job was taking over her life.

Since that day, she has made a conscious decision to leave her work at the office after 5 P.M. She spends at least an hour a night at something strictly entertaining: books, a phone call to a friend, music, television, or simply quiet talk with her husband. They might take a brisk walk or do some exercises. Church on Sunday, for her, is only for the purpose of worship, refreshing her spirit and visiting with good friends. If work is troubling her on a Sunday morning, she prays about it, but tries to turn conversation with friends to other, lighter topics.

In doing all these things, it may seem as if Lauren is *avoiding* difficulties instead of confronting them. But she's found that it's critical to take a respite from stress. She's learned that it's possible to separate work and home life enough so that some times and some tasks are completely insulated from work stress.

For Reflection

How much time did you spend at home in the last week working at job tasks?

Do you find yourself steering conversations at home and at parties to your work issues and problems?

Think about one or two pleasurable activities you might tackle this evening. Gradually increase the time you spend at home on these hobbies, decreasing the amount of time you worry about work.

SELECT YOUR PRIORITIES

No one can be all things to all people at all times without creating serious guilt, anger, bitterness, and disillusionment. Anyone who says it's possible has never tried it.

In More Depth

Filled with optimism in the 1970s, women were told we could be terrific mothers, loving spouses, and up-and-coming career women. We could have it all. Only a cretin would want to settle for less.

But what we found, as we tried to keep the house, raise the kids, minister to our partners, and hold down demanding positions, was that in fact it's virtually impossible to fulfill three completely different roles simultaneously and do any of them well.

The Idea in Action

Ariel is a hospital administrator raising her daughter on her own. There was a time when she thought she could be president of a company while raising the best children and maintaining the best marriage anywhere. She has found that there are just not enough hours in the day to pull this off.

As a result, she's cut back on her expectations. After determining her priorities—her daughter first, her career second, and her home a distant third—she says that today her house is not as clean as she would like, but she savors the time she spends with her child. She enjoys going to work on flextime, and she enjoys making her home pleasant for the two of them. "As for the career ladder," she says, "I've watched too many people climb up only to be knocked down. That aspect of life is no longer a goal."

For Reflection

How many times in the past month have you felt stress, pressure, and anxiety push you past the breaking point?

Do you find yourself running behind schedule and staying up late at night to finish household tasks or work from the office?

List the top three priorities, in order of importance, in your life. Does your schedule accurately reflect these priorities?

LAST ONE UP MAKES THE BED

Divide at-home responsibilities fairly. To take on more than your share at home is no more acceptable than sitting still for job discrimination at work.

In More Depth

One of the biggest sources of irritation between two people with jobs outside the home is the division of labor once the workday is over. In countless insidious ways, this culture reinforces a woman's traditional role as "keeper of the house." Often, women start out a relationship fully intending to equally divide responsibilities at home, but this determination erodes as time passes. Studies have shown that once children arrive, the pressure to play traditional roles increases dramatically.

Suddenly, the woman who mowed the grass while her husband vacuumed the floors ends up doing most of the child care and all the housecleaning. This transformation may be reinforced when two people have different styles of tolerance for untidiness. A man who says he "helps out" or completes tasks assigned him by his partner is not equally sharing in the household responsibilities. Too many times, a woman complains that the job hasn't been performed to her liking.

If you find yourself in this situation, you're still playing the "mother" role, doling out job tasks and overseeing their completion.

In a truly equitable household arrangement, each of you should shoulder half the responsibilities without one partner being "in charge" of seeing that the work is accomplished. You may find it helpful to set up arbitrary rules, such as "The last one up makes the bed" and "Whoever cooks doesn't have to do the dishes." Many couples find that hiring help to clean the house eliminates arguments over who did what.

The Idea in Action

Chris was a freelance auditor who was getting more and more frustrated with the way that the household jobs were getting done. She was doing more and more of them because her husband simply didn't seem to notice that the floor needed to be vacuumed or the sheets needed to be changed. For a while, she simply gritted her teeth and tried to handle all the household tasks after work, including grocery shopping, cooking, cleaning, laundry, and errands. She found herself with so little time left that she was forced to work far into the night to meet her deadlines. She began to resent the fact that her husband could come home after 8 hours and sit down and read or watch TV while she worked all night in her office. On the weekends, he would spend time working on projects he enjoyed around the house, while her time was spent cleaning indoors on jobs she loathed.

Finally, she sat down with her husband and discussed the workload she was carrying and how she felt about the problem. Her husband was genuinely surprised at how much of the work was falling on her shoulders. Because she hadn't complained, he simply took for granted that the chores were being done. The two worked out a weekend schedule so that each was responsible for cleaning a certain number of rooms. They each did their own laundry, and Chris agreed to cook if he agreed to wash the dishes. Now she has time during the early evening to do chores and work, since she isn't feeling obligated to clean the entire house.

For Reflection

Make a list of all the job responsibilities that you do, and that your partner does.

Can you think of ways to divide the work in an equal fashion?

What stops you from discussing how an uneven burden of labor makes you feel?

TAKE TIME FOR YOURSELF

You can't accomplish anything at home or at work if you're running on empty. Taking time for yourself isn't selfish—it's simply good sense.

In More Depth

The "big picture" can be a depressing thing to look at. The outside world may seem menacing and unsafe. Your job and home responsibilities can sometimes build up until the tasks seem insurmountable. Add to these problems ever-present financial worries or child care difficulties, and your life can feel overwhelming. Do you feel that nothing you can do will make a difference? The job *must* get done, the children *must* be fed, the dog *must* be walked, the car *must* be overhauled, the mortgage *must* be paid. Add to these the larger problems of society—drugs, crime, poverty—and it's not surprising that women start feeling helpless, hopeless, and overwhelmed.

At times like these, your own personal space and time become extremely important. By creating harmony where you live and work, by controlling a few hours of your own private time, you can create an oasis of calm in the middle of any hurricane.

The problem is that for too many of us, doing things "just for us" feels selfish. In reality, it's anything but. How can we hope to accomplish anything if we let our mental and physical health fall to pieces? Actually, we all need small moments of space apart—time just for ourselves. Virginia Woolf wrote that "in solitude we give passionate attention to our lives, to our memories, to the details around us." It was true in 1929 when Virginia wrote *A Room of One's Own*, and it's still true today.

The Idea in Action

Dottie worked in a large department store during the day while her daughter was in elementary school. She took on freelance typing assignments in the evenings. Every day she drove her daughter to kindergarten in the next town, worked until early afternoon and then picked up her daughter after school. Back home, she faced an untidy house, breakfast dishes in the sink, and a pile of typing to be done. There were also mountains of laundry, groceries to buy, dinner to prepare, errands to run. Her daughter wanted attention as well, pestering her mother to play games or entertain her.

As the pressures mounted, Dottie's own health began to deteriorate. She was snappish at work, and she often felt as if she were about to explode. Gradually, she came to see that she had no time for herself to relax and recharge her batteries. She decided to set aside an hour for herself each day after work. She provided crayons and books to keep her daughter occupied, and spent this hour each day just for herself: taking a bubble bath, reading a novel, doing watercolors.

Once she got over the guilt of sitting and painting when there were dirty dishes in the sink, she found that she had more energy after her break to attend to tasks. When her daughter realized that after this one hour her mother would be available to play with her each day, she happily learned to amuse herself in the interim.

For Reflection

When was the last time you did something just for yourself in the midst of other responsibilities?

How has your personal health been lately?

Would you expect employees to work without breaks, lunch, or vacations? Why should you?

HIRE PEOPLE YOU TRUST

Hiring people you trust to take care of some of your responsibilities frees you to be more effective at work.

In More Depth

Hire someone else to handle it. Whether it's help to clean your house, cut your grass, or care for your child, if you take the time to hire people you trust to do a good job, you won't have to waste time at work worrying about things at home. You won't have to take time off to get things done, and you'll be able to concentrate fully on the job at hand.

When researchers studied a single man and single woman middle manager, they found interesting differences in the way the two handled their responsibilities at home. The man had his clothes dry-cleaned, hired a cleaning woman, and ate three meals each week in a restaurant. The woman did her own washing, ironing, housecleaning, and cooking.

Most women growing up in the 1950s and 1960s were taught that these household tasks were "women's work" and without even realizing it, many of us still believe we are supposed to do it all. Many women are reluctant to hire household help because it seems like a waste of money to pay someone to do something you're perfectly capable of doing yourself. In fact, *if it's costing you time or concentration on the job, you're far better off paying someone else to handle it.* In the long run, it's probably much cheaper than a psychiatrist or a divorce lawyer.

The Idea in Action

Nancy, 44, works full-time as a surgical nurse in a suburban hospital. After she and her husband adopted a new baby, she decided to place the child in a day care center at the hospital where she worked. She reasoned that a hospital-run center would give excellent care, and this way she would be in the same building and available to see the boy often. But soon the baby was getting so sick from a variety of easily preventable infectious illnesses that Nancy's pediatrician angrily called the day care center herself to complain.

Nancy was so upset about the poor quality of care that she was constantly leaving her job to go check up on the child. When Nancy wasn't physically visiting the center, she was thinking about it and was having trouble concentrating. The nursing supervisor was becoming irritated at her frequent absences and phone calls, and the mistakes she was starting to make during operations.

Finally, Nancy and her husband hired a college-educated mother of two talented, bright, and happy youngsters to watch over their baby. The infections stopped immediately, and Nancy's son loved his new caregiver.

Now that she wasn't worrying about what was or wasn't being done to her son, Nancy was able to concentrate and contribute 100 percent to the job. Her stress level dropped, and she was much better able to handle the ongoing tension of the operating theater. Within a month, she was promoted to head nurse and given new responsibilities and a higher salary.

For Reflection

How often do you spend time on the phone checking up on things?

Have you had to leave your job in the past month to take care of tasks at home?

If you hired good employees, how much time would you save?

Company Politics

ACCEPT THE CREDIT, ACCEPT THE BLAME

Accept the credit when it's earned, but don't run from taking the blame if you're at fault.

In More Depth

Some women find it difficult to accept praise or credit for a job well done. Others find they can never admit a mistake. The ability to do both can go a long way to establishing your own credibility—people will trust you if they know you're forthright.

The Idea in Action

Emily was a new secretary to the top attorney in one of the largest religious organizations in the country. All the other secretaries were terrified of this fierce-looking man of towering intelligence, who tended to bark at his subordinates when they didn't meet with his approval.

A few days after she began working with him, she misplaced an important file on a pending lawsuit. Everyone on the floor could hear him ranting in his office as he searched for the file. The other secretaries huddled behind their computers as Emily walked into his office.

"I'm sorry," she told her boss calmly, who by now was red-faced and furious. "I misplaced that file. I'll spend my lunch hour going through the cabinets."

Apparently astonished at her calm acceptance of the blame, he closed his mouth and even smiled briefly. "Okay. We'll need it as soon as possible." It was clear that when there was a problem, he wasn't interested in excuses—he just wanted the problem to be fixed. Acknowledging blame and proceeding with a plan to solve the problem enhanced Emily's credibility and played a part in her promotion to office manager shortly thereafter.

For Reflection

How many times in the past month have you made a mistake on the job?
How many times did you admit it?
Is it easier for you to accept praise or blame?

IT'S A POLITICAL WORLD

In every job there are politics. Try to understand them. Nothing happens in a corporate vacuum.

In More Depth

No matter how frustrating corporate politics can be, railing about the injustice of it all won't get you anywhere. If the politics are really insupportable, you can always transfer out of the department or get another job.

If you stay, you'll have to understand that the only way to succeed in business is to understand the political scene—who has the power and what his or her objectives are—and play the game accordingly.

The Idea in Action

Cheryl was a successful freelance writer who had just completed a major article for a national woman's magazine. After it was finished, the assigning medical editor called to tell her the piece had been given to the beauty department to edit, and that the beauty editor wanted her to include information about beauty products in the piece.

Cheryl did not miss the definite note of sarcasm in the editor's voice. She knew that taking an article away from one editor and giving it to another was a political hot potato. She could also tell that the editor didn't think much of the beauty editor's journalistic abilities, although she couldn't say so outright. When a fact checker called her a short time later to question her about the piece's tone, Cheryl discovered the new editor had slashed her article to bits and rewritten sections with incorrect information.

Because of the political situation, Cheryl knew she could not call on the original editor for help. It was obvious that the beauty editor did not understand any of the complex medical information, but that the decision to let her edit the piece had come from a superior. By carefully crafting her words, Cheryl was able to steer through the potential minefield without doing major damage to herself, to the fact checker who had alerted her to the changes in the article, or to the original medical editor. "I didn't know why they had switched editors on me," Cheryl recalls, "but I knew something was going on behind the scenes. I was able to deal with everyone so that I didn't burn my bridges with the medical editor, whom I'd like to work with again."

For Reflection

Do you know who holds the real power in your department? In your organization?

List five people in your organization who hold more power than it would seem they wield.

NEVER UNDERSELL YOURSELF

Know what you're worth, and never accept anything less. There's nothing wrong with negotiating for a higher salary, better benefits, or more lucrative bonuses.

In More Depth

From childhood, women are socialized to get along, to give way, and to "be nice." We're trained not to argue, not to boast, not to be aggressive or demanding. Those traits might earn you friends on the playground or plaudits from the teacher, but it won't get you very far in the real world of work.

When you go for a job interview, it's imperative that you know what you're worth and what the company can afford to offer you. If the offer is lower than either of those two figures, it's up to you to demand more, firmly and politely—because if you don't, nobody else will come forward to do so on your behalf.

Of course, "demand" doesn't mean you have to be ugly about it. It's perfectly possible to be polite but firm, to be very sure what it is you are worth and why you won't take a penny less.

The Idea in Action

Kate was a 28-year-old marketing consultant when she and three others of the same age and experience were hired by a new Washington, D.C., professional association to start a public relations department. The salary she was offered was much more than she had been making in her previous job, and she and the other two women accepted their offer eagerly. Kate found out later that the equally qualified male consultant in the group was making more money. Outraged, Kate confronted him about the discrepancy and told him what the women were earning. He seemed surprised.

"They offered me the same money they offered you," he told Kate. "But I asked for more." Kate realized that the fault lay not with the company—after all, she had been offered an equal salary—but with her inability to negotiate on her own behalf. When Kate discussed the matter with the other two women, all agreed that asking for more money had never occurred to any of them. All had assumed that the salary was not negotiable, and all were reluctant to seem "pushy" or "brash" by demanding more money.

For Reflection

Have you ever taken a job that offered a lower salary than you thought you were worth?

How would you feel if you asked for more money the next time?

What's the worst thing that might happen if you did ask for more money?

FOLLOW YOUR OWN STAR

Don't ride anyone else's coattails on the way up the career ladder. It makes for a very slippery position.

In More Depth

We all know company superstars, the Golden Girls who seem as if they can do no wrong. It's tempting to attach ourselves to them, in hopes of basking a bit in reflected glory. But the moral here is that even some of the brightest stars eventually burn up in reentry. If you get a little too close, you run the risk of incinerating yourself as well.

Instead, make career decisions according to your own personal and professional goals. Having mentors and learning from older, more experienced women is fine, as long as you keep your own path firmly fixed in your mind.

The Idea in Action

Danielle was executive assistant in public relations at a national professional association when Jenny came from another state to take over as director of professional development. Recognizing Jenny's power and charisma and correctly guessing she was destined to be the association's rising star, Danielle obtained a transfer to become Jenny's executive assistant.

Each year, Jenny became more and more powerful and Danielle enjoyed promotion after promotion at her side. Unfortunately, as

Jenny clawed her way to the top, she began stepping on toes—lots of toes. As her ego mushroomed, others in high places began to grumble. Then Jenny began an affair with the director of the organization, which served only to fan the flames of dissension and resentment.

Finally, a shake-up on the board of directors led to Jenny's dismissal. Known only as Jenny's right-hand woman, Danielle found herself floundering. By aligning herself so completely with Jenny, she had cut herself off from all other avenues of support. While she did not lose her job, she was allied so closely with the fallen star in others' minds that the new regime did not seem able to trust her.

Danielle eventually quit her job and accepted a position at another organization, where she vowed never to make the same mistake again.

For Reflection

Have you built your own reputation, or are you riding on someone else's wave?

If your boss was fired tomorrow, how secure would your own job be?

Can you identify women in your organization who have allied themselves too closely with another?

STAY OFF THE GRAPEVINE

Focus on the work, not the players. Place principles before personalities.

In More Depth

Don't be too eager to trust any and all female co-workers simply because they are women. Unfortunately, competition is not a gender-specific experience; women are just as capable as men of being less than supportive in their own interests.

For this reason, gossip should have no place in your on-the-job behavior. In the first place, you never know if the person you're gossiping *to* will one day be your supervisor. Gossip always has a way of getting back to the subject of the talk; someday that person may be in a position of authority over you.

Lastly, gossip is often *unfair*. What may be juicy tidbits to you could be grossly inaccurate or just plain false. Spreading untruths is morally wrong and can get downright ugly. If someone were gossiping about you, wouldn't you want co-workers to stand up for you and refuse to spread the dirt?

The Idea in Action

Karen was a hard-working personnel specialist at a large southern medical center. Her department was an all-woman group, and she felt comfortable and friendly with all her co-workers. As part of her job, Karen often had to travel throughout the different departments in the hospital. By necessity, much of her time was spent away from the office. Unbeknownst to her, one of her co-workers had been regularly reporting Karen's "transgressions" to their boss, such as the fact that Karen was taking half-hour catnaps in vacant hospital beds. None of these reports were true.

Unfortunately, Karen did not find out about these false reports until after she had left that job for a better position at another hospital. Her boss had never confronted her with the false accusations, so Karen did not have the opportunity to defend herself. A third co-worker overheard one of these discussions shortly before Karen left, but told Karen about what was happening only afterward. Karen was deeply wounded to think another woman would try to undermine her career.

For Reflection

Have you ever heard an untrue story circulating about you? How did it make you feel?

Think about what you could say the next time someone comes to you with a bit of gossip.

What would happen in your office if you flatly refused to indulge in gossip?

KEEP YOUR EYES AND EARS OPEN

It's easy to get caught up in the emotional side of work. It's important to step back from time to time and evaluate the job, and the company, objectively.

In More Depth

Realize that a company is adept at manipulating your emotions, your competitiveness, loyalty, and pride. You may think that your company is primarily interested in tapping your intellectual skills. Remember that everyone from direct managers to CEOs is going to have motivating words for you, words that collectively form a company story. The company story is about its strengths, its position with its competitors, the esteem in which it is held by customers, and its unique capabilities.

Naturally, the company wants to tell its story in the most positive, most compelling way. Workers for the organization are told that story in part to motivate them to be enthusiastic, competitive, and invested in the company's success.

As one of those workers, you need to distinguish objective from subjective fact. You need to keep informed about what's going on in the world outside the company, and you need to distance yourself from the emotion of the "party line," in order to judge just how true the company's story really is.

Is the company clinging to an image or a product that was valid 10 years ago, but not today? Is it overstating its position in the market-place? Is it asking you to be loyal, proud, or competitive when there is little objective reason to do so? Know when to be analytical and when to be emotional about the needs and goals of the organization, and about your future within it.

The Idea in Action

Anastasia took on a job as editorial consultant for a fledgling publishing company interested in putting out a new, innovative type of business magazine. The publication was not to be sold on newsstands, but as part of an ill-conceived pyramid scheme whose origins and methods were never well delineated. While not well versed in the business world, Anastasia had logged many years of editorial experience and was particularly adept at streamlining tasks.

When she accepted the consultant's position, she was delighted at the salary. Very soon, however, she grew uneasy with many other aspects of the job. The editorial process seemed muddled and illogical, and she was uneasy with many of the employees. The secretary with whom she needed to work closely was related by marriage to the boss, and obviously wanted Anastasia's job for herself, although she was ill equipped to handle it.

Anastasia struggled on in good faith, spending hundreds of hours thinking of ways to improve the magazine and streamline its production. She was more confused when her many solid suggestions were met with silence or puzzled nods. She was therefore not surprised when several months later, the publication abruptly shut down.

It was only later that she learned the company had not been everything it professed to be. Apparently the operation actually served as a cover for questionable, if not downright illegal, activities. The organizational methods and goals had not made sense because in fact the company was not really supposed to succeed.

She vowed that before she accepted the next permanent consulting position, she would ask tough questions about the company's goals, intentions, and backing.

For Reflection

Can you articulate your company's image?

Can you identify the various ways the company tries to manipulate your emotions?

Do your interests and those of the organization conflict?

BE REALISTIC

You may have the education, talent, and skills for the job or promotion, but sometimes that just doesn't matter.

In More Depth

If you work in a corporate structure, odds are you will experience chauvinism. Accept that as reality and don't try to change everyone at once. Don't overreact to comments or you will be perceived as militant. Does this mean you need to swallow insults with a deaf ear and a sweet smile? Not at all.

Be subtle. Don't grandstand. Go about doing the best job you can, and show your worth by setting a good example. Stand up for what you believe in, but choose the time and place to make your point. Don't win the battle and lose the war.

Many women in the corporate world have observed that the atmosphere for women in business was much worse 20 years ago. Men have learned—often the hard way—that sexist comments, rude jokes, and insulting practices are not acceptable.

Still, the problems have not disappeared. If the atmosphere gets really oppressive, you may need to decide whether to stay and fight or jump ship and try another company. "Being a woman can really cripple you in many aspects of your career," says Hope, a midlevel executive. "But at the same time, you can't use chauvinism as an excuse for failure."

The Idea in Action

Kathryn was marketing director of a large New England advertising firm whose peer—an advertising director from the South—appeared to have a problem accepting women in business. Whenever Kathryn asked him something in a meeting, he would respond "Yes, young lady" in a condescending tone. Knowing that the worst thing she could do would be to make a big deal of his tone in the meeting, Kathryn ignored his attitude the first 10 or 20 times. Finally, she met with him privately in his office. "I explained to him politely that I felt uncomfortable with his tone of voice in meetings, and that his condescension undermined my authority."

When he protested that he didn't know what she was talking about, she provided him with three examples she had prepared for the occasion. "He looked at me as if I had three heads," Kathryn recalled. He professed innocence and told her, in a condescending tone, that he certainly didn't realize she felt that way. "I realized I had a sow's ear here, so I didn't expect him to change," Kathryn says now. "But I believed I owed it to myself to let him know he made me feel uncomfortable."

In fact, his attitude change lasted only for one meeting. The next day, he did not use the condescending tone to Kathryn—instead, he chose not to address her at all. After that, he fell back into his old method of communication.

In fact, this man never changed, and Kathryn didn't hold much hope that he would. Rather than push the matter, she chose to let it drop. Widely unpopular in part because of his attitudes, the advertising manager eventually left the company.

"I believe men don't like to be confronted by anyone, but especially by a woman," Kathryn explains. "If you must be confrontational, try to use nonthreatening, nonemotional words and examples."

For Reflection

Did you ever feel diminished because you were a woman?

Imagine a confrontational and a nonthreatening response to an uncomfortable situation. Which would be more effective? Why?

How would you deal with a chauvinistic boss?

DON'T MIX LOVE AND WORK

Never, never, never get involved with a co-worker, a subordinate, or a boss. At best, it's uncomfortable for everyone else, and at worst, it's unethical.

In More Depth

There's a reason that almost every profession has a codified prohibition against getting sexually involved with co-workers or clients. Someone almost always gets hurt.

Of course, it's hard to be objective in the middle of a romantic fantasy, so here are the facts. If you're in a management position, getting involved with a subordinate puts you both in an extremely uncomfortable position. It's a given that eventually, no matter how discrete you are, the rumor mill will be grinding out the news. Other co-workers will be resentful, and suspicious that the favored employee will be unfairly promoted. Romantic disagreements outside of work will disrupt the professional atmosphere. If the relationship goes awry, there are very real legal risks that may result, together with financial settlements and damaging court suits. Innocent flirting may be misconstrued as sexual harrassment.

If you're in a subordinate position, an involvement with the boss is even trickier. This is an especially difficult experience for a young woman just entering the job force, who may in some way feel pressured into an affair.

The Idea in Action

Jim was president of a large insurance firm on the East Coast. Shirley was a talented executive secretary to his vice president of public relations, who was transferred to Jim's office when his own secretary left to have a baby. The two shared many of the same interests and quickly became a team on the job. It wasn't long before Jim was confiding his problems with his wife to Shirley over long lunches, late-night work sessions, and finally dinner at exclusive restaurants around the city. Eventually, they began having an affair.

While they believed they were the picture of propriety, in fact every glance and exchange revealed their intimacy. It wasn't long before everyone in the company knew about the relationship. The atmosphere became difficult, especially when Jim's wife would call and demand to know where her husband was when he was out with Shirley. Staffers became uncomfortable and then angry when they felt they had to lie and cover up. Other secretaries began to resent Shirley's advancements and salary bonuses. They felt she was earning more than she was worth and that her bonuses were earned at their expense.

Finally, Jim's wife confronted him and threatened a divorce, which Jim didn't want. To appease her, he fired Shirley, who promptly filed a grievance against him. She claimed sexual harrassment—a charge that Jim could not defend, since everyone in the building knew about their relationship. Eventually Shirley was given a settlement by the company, but the attitudes against her were so strong she had to leave the firm, where she had accumulated much seniority.

For Reflection

Have you been contemplating an office romance?

Imagine how you would feel if everyone in the building were talking about you. Do you really think you could keep a relationship quiet?

Is a relationship worth the possibility of losing your job?

Working Relationships

MAKE PEOPLE FEEL APPRECIATED

Spend time and attention on your team members. If they feel you have their interest at heart, they'll work with you.

In More Depth

Let's face it—we all like to be appreciated. Your employees are far more willing to put up with occasional long hours, difficult tasks, or unpleasant details if they feel that their efforts are noticed. It's especially important not to neglect your star players—those folks you can always count on to get the job done, on time and in perfect order.

Are you neglecting those folks in favor of the ones who need prodding and pushing? Are you rewarding solid performance by additional responsibilities? Remember that no one likes to be taken for granted, and eventually those who are will leave if they feel they aren't appreciated.

Remember that it takes far less time and money to express or reward appreciation to excellent employees than it does to recruit, hire, and train their replacements.

The Idea in Action

Harriet was a management trainee in a large auto rental agency. In the last several weeks, she'd been putting in a number of late nights in order to implement a new computerized business system that her boss had been developing. There were quite a few bugs to be worked out, and since Harriet's specialty was computers, she'd been called on to provide her expertise on top of her other duties.

After she'd put in an entire weekend on the plan, she came to work tired and demoralized. The computer system was a success, but Harriet was totally exhausted. She wasn't sure all her extra work was really going to be rewarded or even noticed. On her chair, she noticed a small piece of white note paper, folded over. It was a handwritten note from her boss, expressing how much she'd appreciated Harriet's dedication and efforts on behalf of the plan. Harriet carried the note around with her for days, and would peek at it on days when things were rough.

Harriet later learned that her boss often expressed her appreciation this way, in brief notes left discreetly on employees' desks. Her boss had learned that while verbal thanks are certainly valuable, a written note of appreciation has even more impact; it can be savored and reread.

For Reflection

Can you name the top best producers among your employees?

How many times have you told them they were appreciated in the last month?

Contrast this with how much time you've spent on the bulk of your middle-of-the-road workers.

ACCEPT OTHERS AS THEY ARE

Understand the personality styles of your team members. Every organization needs diversity—learn to capitalize on co-workers' strengths and accept their weaknesses.

In More Depth

Since every individual brings a unique perspective to the workplace, it's a safe bet that you'll find all sorts of personalities among co-workers. It's just not realistic to expect everyone to get along, all the time. For this reason, it's important to learn everyone's strengths and weaknesses, and *not to expect too much.* When you know how others in your group will react, you won't be disappointed.

It's particularly important not to put yourself in the position of being dependent on someone else who can't follow through for personal reasons. Maybe you're working with someone on an important investment strategy—but your co-worker has a procrastination problem. Depending on that person to turn in her share of the work could jeopardize the whole project and *both* your reputations.

The Idea in Action

Cindy was a young city magazine editor whose close friend, Mary, was hired as a cub reporter. While Cindy was not responsible for directly supervising her friend, there were occasions when Mary would be responsible for writing an article for Cindy's magazine.

Each week Cindy was on a tight deadline and any delays would bring down the wrath of the shop foreman on her head. An organized perfectionist, Cindy always had all her material in order and ready for printing by her deadline—except when Mary was writing a story.

A graduate of a top university, Mary was brilliant but erratic, and an inveterate procrastinator. Time after time, Mary would be pecking out her story on the computer as the shop supervisor was ranting to Cindy in the next room.

Cindy valued the woman's abilities, but realized that Mary was simply incapable of meeting a deadline. Unwilling to lose a talented writer, Cindy simply worked around Mary's shortcomings. She issued artificial deadlines. She built up her inventory of other stories so that she always had other choices if Mary's pieces were turned in too late to run that week. By utilizing these ploys, she was able to work around Mary's foibles while maintaining her own sanity.

For Reflection

What are the strengths and weaknesses of your employees?

Can you think of some creative ways you can work around those weaknesses?

In what ways have other bosses you've had been aware of their employees' pluses and minuses? How did this relate to their effectiveness?

PRESERVE YOURSELF

Don't allow anyone to take advantage of you. Learn about group dynamics and how to handle dysfunctional group members.

In More Depth

A woman's tendency to be nice and not make waves puts her in real danger of being taken advantage of. This is a particular problem for younger women just entering the work force who are especially eager to do well and advance in their career.

Listen.

Observe.

Dysfunction in group members is a reality. A boss with a substance abuse problem and a temper who gets drunk at lunch can cause all sorts of problems. You probably feel as if you can't do anything about it, or risk losing your job.

It may not always be easy to recognize when that person has a dysfunction. Mental health issues that may not be as obvious as alcoholism can be just as detrimental to team morale.

The Idea in Action

Kara was a young congressional assistant who had been hired fresh out of college. She was thrilled to be working in Washington, even though her salary was quite low and barely covered her living expenses.

As young as she was, it didn't take her long to realize that morale in the office was shockingly low. There always seemed to be an under-current of angry buzzing. She began to notice that after lunch, many of her office co-workers tended to disappear, inventing all sorts of excuses to be out of the office. She was therefore often alone when her boss came back from lunch, none too sober. It became apparent that his excessive drinking, mixed with a nasty temper, became a real problem for any hapless employee he happened to run across when he returned from lunch.

For several months, Kara took the abuse. She felt it would look bad on her résumé if she quit her job so soon after being hired, and she really needed the money. But on the day her boss raked her over the coals for not carrying through a task he had actually assigned to someone else, she decided that no job was worth the abuse she was taking.

On the basis of contacts she'd made while on staff in Congress, she got a job as public relations director for a small college in the con-gressman's district and quit his office the same day.

For Reflection

Can you identify any of your co-workers who could be considered dysfunc-tional?

How does their problem affect the rest of the employees?

Short of quitting your job, can you think of a way to handle the problem?

HAVE A MENTOR

Mentor relationships can be invaluable, especially in first or new jobs. A mentor can recognize your potential, challenge you to take risks, and show you, by example, possible paths.

In More Depth

Working women must evaluate periodically whether they need a mentor if they don't have one, whether they've grown beyond a mentor relationship if they do have one, and whether it's time to *become* a mentor to someone else.

While mentors are certainly helpful for anyone in the working world, they are of particular importance to women. A mentor can provide a valuable role model—something that many working women who grew up before the 1970s didn't have. Somewhat different from a friend, role models show us how to handle ourselves in the often-unfamiliar landscape of work—partly by their advice and partly by their own example. Friends are supportive when we make mistakes; mentors show us the way, like a map through a minefield, to avoid the mistakes before we make them.

The Idea in Action

When Sylvia first went to work as an administrative assistant at a large medical center, she was totally naive about the political world of work. Fortunately for her, she was soon transferred to the office of Joan, a rising star in the hospital's human resources department. This polished, poised, and charming older woman was blessed with a sharp mind, a ready wit, and an excellent education. Trained as an attorney, she had chosen the business world of nonprofit hospital administration and seemed to thrive in the deadly political arena there.

Joan had come to power in the wake of massive restructuring of the hospital. The hospital board had swept through the ranks, firing many leaders and promoting others. Sylvia was intimidated at first, but Joan took her under her wing and the two began working closely together.

Under Joan's tutelage, Sylvia quickly learned the ins and outs of the hospital's political scene—who had the real power, who was a figurehead, and why. She learned how to stay out of trouble and how to attract the right kind of attention.

Within 3 years, she had risen to director of one of the largest departments in the hospital, despite a decided prejudice against women in upper management. She would never have come so far, she says now, if it had not been for the advice and guidance all along from her mentor, Joan.

For Reflection

Do you have someone older and more experienced to whom you can turn for advice?

Have you worked in the job long enough to become a mentor yourself?

What kinds of insights and details would you look for in a mentor relationship?

MANAGEMENT IS NOT A FAMILY

You don't have to be liked; you only have to be respected.

In More Depth

Try not to be concerned with what others in the workplace think of you. You will not be liked by everyone. The very fact that you're in management means that sometimes you'll have to make tough decisions. Sometimes, not everyone will like or agree with those decisions. This isn't always easy and won't always come naturally, especially for many women who have been raised with the social imperative that *you must be liked at all costs.*

Women tend to operate by establishing consensus and building relationships. Even in a business environment, women seek to establish mutual agreement, whereas men tend to be more autocratic. Because women find it more natural to establish relationships, maintaining a distance can feel more awkward.

In one study, sets of two same-sex children who didn't know each other were placed in a room with only two chairs, and told to wait. The boys—even the very youngest—did not interact with each other at all. In some cases, the boys placed their chairs facing *away* from each other and sat there, back to back. But in every case, the two girls immediately began to speak to each other in friendly ways. Their chairs were placed *facing* each other—often side by side.

From the cradle, girls are taught by our society to cooperate, not to compete. When these girls grow up, many retain a need to be seen as friendly. Many of these women feel uncomfortable, at least in the beginning, in maintaining a social distance from employees.

You can tell that you've crossed the line between "boss" and "friend" if you find yourself questioning a business decision because it might interfere with a personal relationship with an employee. Remember that you were given a management position to do the job, not to win a popularity contest.

The Idea in Action

Amelia was a midlevel manager at a small building products firm. She worked closely with her assistant, and they had many mutual interests. Although Amelia genuinely liked her assistant, she chose to keep their relationship on a professional basis because she was responsible for her reviews, promotions, and raises.

The time came when Amelia needed to be more stern than usual with her assistant during a review in order to correct a behavior that she felt was not appropriate. Because Amelia could be professional, logical, and divorced from emotional feelings, the review was much easier to do. Amelia didn't have to preface her remarks by saying, "Okay, I can't be your friend now, I have to be your boss." It was understood that she was a boss and not a friend, and the reproof was taken in the professional manner in which it was given. Since that time, both women have left the company and are now friends who do things together socially. The assistant has told Amelia she was the best boss she ever had.

For Reflection

Do you worry what co-workers think of you?
Do you have trouble disciplining or firing employees?
Are you more comfortable being a pal or a boss?

Leadership

SMELL THE ROSES

Doing a good job is important, but don't lose sight of everything else in your drive to excel.

In More Depth

Many women commit everything to their job in an effort to get ahead, spending huge amounts of time on the job. But even if you put all your energies into a corporation where you have little real security, you may end up being "downsized" anyway.

It's important to keep your job in perspective, and to understand that the extra time spent on your job may or may not be rewarded. You need to do other positive things for yourself, whether that is dating, playing with your kids, going to the theater, exercising, shopping, or playing golf. Try to maintain balance, keeping your job and all your other interests in perspective. Don't sacrifice other things that are important for the sake of your job, because your job may not support you in the end.

The Idea in Action

Elizabeth P. was the assistant comptroller of a large corporation, where she regularly put in 60-hour weeks. Consumed by her job, she had no time during the week to go out and socialize and do fun things. This caused a fair amount of stress and anxiety. Being single, she wasn't meeting other people; she had no dating life and no time for herself to attend the ballet or musical performances.

For 8 years, she worked at least 60 hours a week and got outstanding reviews—and then got laid off anyway when her company was taken over by another firm. "If you look back on it, I could have probably done the job in 40 to 50 hours a week," Elizabeth says, "and had 10 extra hours to do fun things."

She now believes that downsizing was a blessing, because she found a new job making more money and working fewer hours than she ever did at her last job. She has gotten married and spends her weekends decorating her new home, traveling, and attending the ballet, which she loves.

For Reflection

When was the last time you did something impulsive, just for you?

Think of five things that you'd love to do but think you just don't have time for.

Imagine how you would schedule your day so that you could do at least one of those things, once or twice a week.

ASSERT YOURSELF!

If you want to get the job done, you'll need to be assertive.

In More Depth

Conflicting male-female leadership styles can cause problems for women in management. Women use the language of rapport in negotiation, believing that the way to achieve a common goal is to gain consensus. We seek connectedness, consensus, and cooperativeness among group participants.

On the other hand, men in the business world often misjudge this behavioral style. They interpret any interest in consensus as insecurity, weakness, and incompetence. Many men may view this behavior as an inability to lead.

The Idea in Action

Jean was a project team leader at a cellular phone company. She ran meetings as a discussion group, seeking idea sharing and consensus in decision making. She was shocked when her male mentor, who attended these sessions, suggested that she appeared to lack the authority necessary to run the team.

At first Jean bristled at her mentor's assessment. But then she read some popular books about the different communication styles of men and women in business, and she began to realize that her mentor was simply interpreting her own style in a way consistent with his view of the business world. Since most of her group members were men, Jean realized that in order to be successful, she would need to incorporate at least some aspects of this foreign behavior pattern.

With the help of some good books and a few sessions of role playing with members of her women's business group, Jean learned how to be more assertive and directive as the team leader, although she did not entirely abandon her comfortable style. She sensed that, indeed, her altered leadership style resulted in more respect from the male members of her group.

For Reflection

When someone cuts in front of you in line or tries to get waited on first, are you able to speak up or do you fume in silence?

How would you describe your leadership style: aggressive, assertive, or consensual?

Imagine a confrontation at work. Can you mentally rehearse an assertive response to the situation? What did you learn from it?

BE FLEXIBLE

Women often have to juggle a wide range of responsibilities at home and at work. Whether or not that's fair is irrelevant here. The fact is, it often happens. So how can you deal with it?

In More Depth

To be effective at home and on the job, you've got to learn to be flexible. Always try to think ahead to the next thing that needs to be done, and try to learn to shift gears smoothly from one task to the next. This is particularly important for women with at-home businesses, especially if there are children in the home at the same time. Still, if you have a multitude of responsibilities you will find that flexibility helps you make use of *all* your time. You'll get more done with less anxiety if you're capable of changing direction rapidly.

Some women are naturally more flexible than others. Rigid, perfectionistic personalities with great power of concentration and focus may find it difficult to rapidly shift attention from one task to the next. These women tend to work on one thing at a time, focusing intently on the project at hand until its completion, and then moving on.

While the ability to be flexible in part is inborn, you can try to practice this skill and apply it to home and work situations.

The Idea in Action

Kirsten quit her teaching job to stay home and raise her two girls, a 4 year old and a 1 year old, and start a home-based educational software company. She uses e-mail and the Internet to stay connected with other professionals and to keep up with current technology should she eventually decide to return to the corporate world.

Because she has found it difficult to concentrate on involved, in-depth work project issues while the girls nap during the day, she breaks down the tasks she needs to accomplish with her business. The small, easily-accomplished duties she reserves for nap time, and saves the jobs that need complete uninterrupted attention for the evening. Household tasks are wedged in during moments when she cannot work effectively.

For Reflection

Do you find it easy to change gears and move from one task to another?

Make a list of several jobs you need to accomplish. Can you break them down into smaller steps?

Think about the most effective, organized person in your work group. How well does she move from one task to the next?

PLAY ON YOUR STRENGTHS

What you do well is what you ought to be doing. Playing on your strengths is manipulation of the best kind.

In More Depth

We all have strengths we are proud of and weaknesses that we wish no one else would ever find out about. In the working world, it pays to take advantage of the fact that without a doubt, there is something that you likely do very well. Why not concentrate on that, and side-step those personal drawbacks that you'd like to forget about?

The Idea in Action

Diane was hired as an office assistant in training and development for a large corporation. She came on board just when the company was eliminating its mainframe computer in favor of a line of individual PCs for all employees.

Diane was sent off to a week-long workshop on computer operation, and came back to work completely fascinated with the new technology. Soon, all the other secretaries were coming to her whenever they had a problem with the system. Diane read and explored on her own time, getting books out of the library, subscribing to magazines, and haunting computer stores. She was fascinated with the computer and what it could do for her on the job.

When Diane was promoted to editor of the employee newsletter, her love of the computer made her job even easier. But she hated editing and writing, and—a hopeless procrastinator—she found the endless deadlines distressing. Each day, she longed to be left alone so she could work out new solutions with the computer. She quickly realized that her inability to meet deadlines could be a real drawback to an editor of a newsletter, but her affinity for computers was a definite strength that could be put to use in the company.

When the firm decided to create a computer department to handle its on-line needs, Diane was able to show her superiors that her computer literacy made her the obvious choice to head up the group. Today, she's doing a job she loves and getting paid for having fun—all because she played up her strengths.

For Reflection

Is your current job utilizing your strengths or exploiting your weaknesses?

Would you be happier in a different position in your job?

What's holding you back?

LEARNING NEVER STOPS

Whatever your field, you can't afford to let your profession pass you by. Learning doesn't stop once you leave school. There are always things to learn that will help you on the job.

In More Depth

The day you stop learning is the day you begin to lose your place in the working world. Sound overly dramatic? It's not. Ask any scientist, lawyer, or physician whether she put away the books after university, and she'll tell you that was only the beginning. Continuing education credits, workshops, conferences, professional journals—the learning never stops.

Continuing to develop the skills you need to get along in your job will benefit you in the long run. Not only will you obtain information you can use every day on the job, but in this era of corporate downsizing, a woman who hasn't kept current may find it much harder to locate a new job after a layoff or takeover.

The Idea in Action

Ten years ago, Jenny was starting out as an organizational psychologist in a midwestern state. As do most other professionals, she used a small personal computer for business correspondence, patient records, and tax information. But 2 years ago when her company was sold to a much larger firm, she realized that many of her new colleagues were far more computer literate than she was.

In one recent meeting, everyone else was discussing new types of programs and applications in ways she had never considered. She hadn't had time to keep up with the journals and professional newspapers that had been outlining these changes and how computer communication was remaking her world. She listened to the others discuss the latest research they had been downloading from the Internet and other on-line sources. Jenny had nothing to say and nothing to offer. She realized that the scenario would be repeated at any other company, and that her solution was not to hide her head under her computer table, but to learn a lot about computers in a hurry.

She decided to attend a seminar she'd heard about that was designed to help people become familiar with all the new computer systems and services. She bought an entire new system and spent several weekends boning up on terminology. At the next company meeting, she was able to advise co-workers about an interesting bulletin board she'd heard about at the conference. Jenny has learned that keeping up with the latest technology is the surest way to guarantee her own employability.

For Reflection

When was the last time you really read some of those professional publications that come across your desk?

Are you doing everything you can to keep up with the new information and technology in your career?

Think about attending at least one job-related conference a year. What could you learn from them?

BELIEVE IN YOURSELF

Make your steps small enough so you can accomplish your goal with minimal strain. Don't decide how large a step to take on the basis of what you believe you should accomplish.

In More Depth

All too many of us have been raised with the unspoken message that to be a woman means to defer, to be modest, to acquiesce. Even when parents try to raise their daughters without these messages, research shows that not only does society (books, TV, movies) uphold the stereotypes—*it can have more impact on the child than parents have themselves.*

Discounting our skills—believing it's luck, not ability—is an attitude many women hold. Women who don't believe in their talent are less likely to make commitments to it. If they do, they feel as if they're fooling everyone.

Don't discount your success, and don't focus on your weakness and ignore your strength. Believe in your own ability and resist the tendency to get "stuck" in your career or your life.

The Idea in Action

Susan was a 37-year-old advertising executive who lived in fear of the moment her boss discovered she was a fraud. Although others saw her remarkable ability and flair for business, Susan knew better. Despite her advanced degree and extensive sales experience, she believed she landed her present job by a combination of luck and charm. She hesitated to take on more responsibility, fearing she'd fail. She couldn't leave the company, because who else would believe she could do the job?

Susan was stuck. Her internal obstacles were not real; she couldn't explain or even fully understand them. She just knew that she walked around most of the time feeling anxious. Fortunately for Susan, her older sister had worked through many of the same problems. After a long talk one night, her sister explained that taking action was the antidote to her anxiety. "Baby steps," her sister advised. "Just take baby steps."

One by one, Susan began to set goals and plan how to achieve them. When her boss gave her a new account, instead of panicking Susan calmly sat down and wrote out her goals. She broke down each goal into smaller steps to help her clarify what needed to be done. She began keeping a daily diary to track how she spent her time, and where things began to break down. Before beginning each new goal, she would mentally go over each part of the activity and its outcome. As she began meeting each small goal, her self-confidence grew.

She made a self-management chart for each day of the week, and at the end of each day she checked off each job she had completed. "It was an unbelievably great feeling to see how many jobs I had accomplished," she reported. As each major goal was met, she rewarded herself with a new book.

For Reflection

Do you feel as if you don't deserve your present success?
What method do you use to track your goals?
How do you make sure your visions are achieved?

STEER YOUR OWN SHIP

You are in control of your own life, your own future. If you start relying on the approval of others, you'll lose your way.

In More Depth

A famous basketball star was asked how he managed to play when the fans booed him when he made a mistake. "I don't hear the boos," he explained, "because I don't hear the cheers." What this athlete had learned was that if you rely too much on the opinions of others, you lose control of your own happiness. For him, this meant that he tuned out the praise as well as the criticism, because he realized that this feedback was coming from *outside* himself. What really counts is how you feel about yourself.

This doesn't mean that you should ignore valuable feedback or fail to acknowledge praise. Just don't let it take over your life. If you've gone too far in the other direction—if you start worrying about the opinions of others to the exclusion of your own good sense—it's time to readjust your focus.

A woman who relies too heavily on others' opinions won't be able to take the calculated risks that are sometimes necessary if real growth is to occur. Who can dare to risk, when she's worried about how those actions will be perceived? The problem begins to feed on itself, as your world narrows farther and farther, until finally it may be difficult to take any action at all for fear of alienating some ill-defined "other" outside yourself.

The Idea in Action

Vickie was an extremely capable biophysicist working in a research lab at a well-known university. Her work was first-rate, but her department head noticed that while she was clearly brilliant, her papers tended to be rather pedestrian. She chose to focus on small side issues and rarely initiated her own research. When she had an opportunity to present an important paper at a professional conference, she backed out.

Concerned about her diffident manner, her boss questioned Vickie about what was going on. In the face of her boss's obvious concern, Vickie finally admitted that she lived in fear of her colleagues' condemnation. She had seen co-workers' papers presented at professional conferences come under attack—or so she saw it—by other scientists for everything from study design to conclusions. Vickie was so worried about what colleagues might say about her work that she was unable to design challenging studies that might attract the attention of others.

Vickie was setting herself up to fail—or at least, not to progress in her career—out of a fear of how others might judge her work. Once she realized how seriously this problem was affecting her career, she resolved to address the situation. She began attending speakers' groups for practice in public speaking. She took an assertiveness training course and engaged in extensive role playing with her boss on how to anticipate and parry critical questions about her research.

With her boss's help, she began presenting small papers at workshops, then small conferences, gradually working her way up to more prestigious organizations. While she will probably never really love this part of her job, by recognizing the importance of attending to her inner beliefs about her work, Vickie has been far more successful in her career.

For Reflection

Which do you tend to remember—a compliment or a criticism?

When someone criticizes your work, how does that make you feel? What is your response?

What can you say to yourself the next time someone criticizes your work so you don't take the comments to heart?

DON'T LET FEAR GET IN YOUR WAY

"Be bold! If you're going to make an error, make it a doozy, and don't be afraid to hit the ball."

—*Billie Jean King*

In More Depth

Fear can be crippling. Many women become stressed out in the face of anxiety, and society has often permitted them to avoid challenges. If you don't learn to approach problems with the sense that they can be solved, you'll come to believe that stress and anxiety are the signals to drop what you're doing and run.

Psychologists call this behavior pattern "approach-avoidance." It can lead to either a specific phobic reaction toward a particular task or a general feeling of being "stuck," unable to proceed. This is a particular problem for self-employed women. Without a boss and with no one outside themselves in authority, their work may come to a complete halt.

Those who work for others usually continue doing the job on a basic level, because they are supervised. But when it comes to taking the initiative to move up the corporate ladder or leave for a better job, they can run into trouble. These women sit idle. They don't ask for more challenges. They can't get their résumés together to look for a job.

Fortunately, being "stuck" is not a lifetime sentence; you can work your way out of the rut by taking action to overcome the feeling of helplessness. There is always something you can do: If you see one option, assume there are at least three others. Set goals and plan how to achieve them.

The Idea in Action

Carrie was a pharmacy clerk who was dissatisfied with her present job at a small city drugstore. She knew of three jobs she could apply for and probably get. But instead of copying résumés and writing cover letters, she would suddenly remember phone calls that had to be made, a cake that needed to be baked, laundry that couldn't be put off. She avoided the tasks she knew she needed to tackle in order to find a new job, because she found them overwhelming.

Rather than sitting at her desk thinking about the jumble of things that needed to be done, she decided to concentrate on just one small step at a time, starting with addressing one envelope for one of the job possibilities on her list. Once she had the envelopes out and one envelope addressed, it took only a small act of courage to address the next one.

Carrie started small—addressing an envelope—because she knew the much larger task of rewriting a résumé and getting it printed was more intimidating for her. She broke the résumé job down into parts—rewriting one small section at a time.

When the résumé was written and typed, she made a date with herself to drop it off at a copy shop on her way to having lunch with her best friend. This way, the odious task was combined with a pleasant reward and increased the chances of actually following through.

Carrie found that as she accomplished the small steps of her plan, the positive reinforcement tended to carry her forward. As she built up momentum, it became easier and easier to just keep going. Within a week, all her résumés were mailed off and several job interviews were scheduled. She had faced her fears and worked through them.

For Reflection

Are there any job-related tasks that you have been avoiding? Ask yourself why.

Examine your fears for evidence of exaggeration. What's the worst that could happen?

Sit down and plan how you could break up tasks you've been avoiding into smaller steps—the smaller the better.

Techniques

REWARD YOURSELF

Reinforcing achievement is a good way to give yourself recognition for your accomplishments. Even the smallest step should earn a reward.

In More Depth

In an ideal world, all your efforts and achievements would receive recognition and rewards. Unfortunately, this doesn't always happen. But if you work your heart out and receive little in the way of verbal or tangible recognition of that effort, it's easy to start experiencing nagging doubts. Research suggests that women in particular are prone to excessive self-doubt and self-criticism.

Instead of depending on rewards from others, there's nothing wrong with giving yourself a pat on the back for a job well done. Did you meet the productivity goals? Did you get your report in on time? Did you complete a stellar portfolio for the investors' meeting?

Buy yourself that book you've been wanting to read, and give yourself time to dip into it. Go out for a decadent lunch with a friend. Treat yourself to a small pleasure you wouldn't ordinarily spend time or money on: a beautiful watercolor, unusual lingerie, an art film.

The Idea in Action

Charlotte was happy in her job as executive assistant at an accounting firm, but her position required that she complete many small daily tasks and small reports. Bright and articulate, Charlotte was also a bit of a procrastinator. The more important the task, the more excuses

Charlotte found not to begin. When she realized her procrastination was starting to cause problems with her boss, she knew she needed to find a way to break her habit.

Charlotte never spent money on luxuries, the legacy of a deprived childhood, although as an adult she could well afford them. Therefore, she decided to give herself "permission" to buy a small scented soap or lotion each time she finished a project. While the actual cost of these items was not high, they had always seemed too frivolous in the past.

Charlotte was amazed at how the thought of "being allowed" to buy another small soap for herself was enough to spur her on to complete her tasks. Within 2 weeks, her boss was complimenting her on her new industriousness, and she was so thrilled with her new purchases that she was psychologically able to accept her on-the-job duties.

For Reflection

When was the last time you rewarded yourself for a job well done?

Can you identify a job you've put off that might get done if you offered yourself a reward?

Make a list of tangible or intangible things you could offer yourself for future rewards.

DON'T DEAL WITH HOME AT WORK

Give the kids some of the responsibilities, or hire responsible people to run your errands, clean your home, cut your grass. Then stand back and let them do the jobs you don't have time for.

In More Depth

Having to juggle home and work tasks isn't necessarily a negative thing, so don't let your company try to convince you it is. There *are* benefits from having both a job and a family. According to Supreme Court Justice Sandra Day O'Connor, "Having family responsibilities and concerns just has to make you a more understanding person on the job."

Of course, that doesn't mean it's easy. It's not fair to your employers if you spend hours on the phone dealing with problems at home. This is when you'll need to develop a strong cadre of support people to help you take care of responsibilities outside of work.

The Idea in Action

Linda, a single mom, was a librarian at a university library who was getting bogged down with nagging tasks at home. The day she realized she needed help, her aging washing machine broke down and the repair person could tell her only that he'd be there "sometime after 10 A.M." Her grass badly needed to be cut, dishes were piled in the sink, and the bathroom hadn't been cleaned in a month. She had laundry to be picked up at the dry cleaners, and she needed to buy a present for her daughter to take to a birthday party that weekend.

"Something just snapped as I stood there in the kitchen arguing with the repairman," she recalls. "I wondered how other people got their washers fixed. I figured they must have someone to stay at home all day and wait for things to be delivered or repaired."

That very day, Linda hired a cleaning service and a lawn service to come to her home once a week. Living in a city, she was able to take advantage of a Rent-a-Housewife service, hiring people to run errands, buy presents, pick up dry cleaning, and take the dog to the vet. "Paying people to do these jobs is a stretch for me, but I'd rather come home to a clean house and neat yard than spend money on dinner and a movie."

For Reflection

How many times in the last week did you have to stop working on a task in order to deal with a problem at home?

Do you feel that being a woman means your role is to do all the laundry, shopping, and cooking?

What would happen if you asked family members to redivide the household chores?

JUST SAY NO

Life is a balancing act. Far too many people climb up the ladder only to get knocked down again. If you can't do it all, you'll have to pick and choose.

In More Depth

Feeling overwhelmed? It's one of the hallmarks of stress, when you contemplate all your varied responsibilities and the limited time in which they must be accomplished. The feeling of being overwhelmed is an indication that you're probably trying to do too much, and you need more structure in the time you do have.

It's not easy to say "no" when people ask you to volunteer your time for worthwhile projects. It's even harder when your boss wants you to put in more hours on the job. It's probably hardest when you feel you should put in more hours of work in your own business.

Still, if you're to maintain any vestige of sanity, you need to do just that. Actually, learning how to say no is really an act of courage. It means you're marshaling the inner strength to make a stand—to tell yourself and others what's important in your life. To do that, you have to be very clear what *is* important in your life, and accept that this end will justify the possible price of saying no.

The Idea in Action

Holly is an airline attendant who has learned the value of saying no. For 20 years, she has worked for a major national air carrier while balancing school and the needs of four children. With the years has come the wisdom of understanding that sometimes, she needs to take care of personal business.

"I take a mental health day off, or even an hour or two that's just for me. I need the time to rejuvenate." She finds that sometimes the pressure of having to perform, plus care for four children, is just too much. She stands back and assesses. She organizes and prioritizes. "I realized that the most important things in my life are my kids, and my own mental and emotional well-being." She turns down extra work and volunteer activities, and takes a walk, visits or calls a friend, listens to music, does repetitive needlework, works out at a gym, takes a long shower, lets her mind wander. By learning to say no, she says yes to life, to things she feels really matter.

For Reflection

How many times in the past week have you felt overwhelmed?

What would happen if you cut back your work hours and trimmed volunteer activities?

Ten years from now, what do you think will be important to you?

KNOW WHEN TO LET GO

Release the unimportant "shoulds." Since you can't possibly do everything perfectly, learn to let some of the less important tasks slide.

In More Depth

It's not possible to have it all. Since no one is perfect at any task, trying to be perfect in three or four major areas of responsibility can't help but fail. Since many women already carry around plenty of guilt for even *trying* to combine job and family, the additional guilt that inevitably follows when you fail to perform all your tasks flawlessly can be crippling.

An alternative approach is to take a good, hard look at your responsibilities. Delegate those important tasks that *must* be done, but that don't have to be done by *you*. Evaluate which of those tasks can be eliminated. If you're having a party, do you *really* need to dust behind the armoire? If you're snowed under at work, do you *really* need to reorganize all your files? Do you *really* need to fold up all the laundry, or could you assign your 10-year-old the job?

One key is to change the way you think about your multiple roles. Instead of telling yourself that you can't possibly keep up with all your responsibilities at home and work, try telling yourself to focus on just those tasks that are important to home and family. The others don't matter. Let them go.

The woman who learns to pare down to the essentials is the woman who is bound to learn more about life, love, and laughter.

The Idea in Action

Susan is a former stewardess now working her way through law school. The mother of four children, she was beginning to crack under the strain of keeping the house clean, maintaining her law studies, attending class, working a part-time job, and keeping the household running. Finally, on the night before an exam when the dishwasher broke and her daughter was upset that her favorite blouse hadn't been washed, Susan broke down. Her family was astounded at the explosion, since she had never let on how much of a strain she was feeling.

After discussing the problem, Susan drew up a plan to rearrange responsibilities. Now, the house gets cleaned on the weekend by the whole family. Dinner chores are shared; she cooks, the kids set and clear the table, wash and dry the pots, load the dishwasher, and take out the garbage. Everyone cleans his or her room before going off for the day. Her husband does the laundry and food shopping, and nothing gets ironed until it needs to be worn.

By letting go of trying to have it all—an immaculate home, perfect kids, a loving relationship, and a fulfilling, successful career—she was able to focus on what matters most. For Susan, this meant letting go of her need for a spotless house and elaborate, gourmet meals in favor of slightly disheveled kids, a fulfilling career, and a great relationship.

For Reflection

Do you try to "have it all"?
Do you feel consumed with guilt or burdened with too much pressure?
What task or responsibility could you delegate to someone else?

ONE THING AT A TIME

Deal with one thing at a time, do it very well, and then move on. Concentrate on dealing with what's at hand at the moment.

In More Depth

Being "bogged down" is only a state of mind—your schedule is what *you* make it. Set your priorities and stick to them. If you feel you are under pressure, learn to delegate to others when you can.

Some people intentionally like to pile up as many projects as they can. "I work better under pressure," they say. All too often, however, this deadline madness backfires. By deliberately telling yourself you work better under pressure, you become more vulnerable. If anything goes wrong—the computer breaks down, the printer runs out of ink, the package delivery is late—what had been "deadline pressure" becomes "uncontrolled emergency."

Some people work this way because they enjoy working at the center of a whirlwind—it makes them feel important. Others have built this style into such a habit that it actually feels *comfortable*.

The Idea in Action

Elizabeth is a Massachusetts stained-glass artist who has learned to handle the pressure of her own business by taking things one at a time. She found herself getting overwhelmed when faced with having to create pieces for a big show. When the pressure builds, she tries to focus on the piece she is working on to the exclusion of everything else. She does one thing at a time, blocking everything else out.

"I found that whatever I did in my other careers, things worked best when I took them one thing at a time, one day at a time." In the past, she felt overwhelmed when faced with a multitude of projects and deadlines. One day she realized she would have to learn how to shield herself from these pressures or she would soon not be able to create anything at all. She learned how to take a step back and tell herself: "Today, I am going to work on this, and this, and this." By calmly setting out a schedule for herself at the beginning of the day covering things she wanted to accomplish, she was able to focus and block out much of the annoying pressure.

For Reflection

How many times in the last week have you felt overwhelmed?

Do you often find yourself juggling a multitude of projects and deadlines?

Think of three ways you could deal with this pressure the next time it occurs.

DON'T FEAR FAILURE

The only person who never failed is someone who never aspired to great things. Take a risk. Dare to fail.

In More Depth

Give yourself permission to fail. It doesn't make you a loser. If you can't accept failure, you won't allow yourself to take any risks, and you'll limit your achievement. Writer Madeleine L'Engle had two well-received books under her belt when she began her third book, a children's story with a very unusual style and treatment. The book was not typical of the times. It used lots of hard words and difficult concepts. Madeleine's own children loved it, and she believed in the work fiercely.

But publisher after publisher turned it down.

"Too unusual."

"Too strange."

"Too challenging."

Knowing full well she might fail, Madeleine refused to alter the story to make it more palatable to the publishers. After 2 years, the manuscript was bought by an editor of a major house, who didn't want her to change a word. The book went on to win the Newbery Award for Children's Literature. Later on, an editor from a rival house gushed over the book and told Madeleine she wished she'd had the opportunity to read *"A Wrinkle in Time"* first. "You did," Madeleine told her. "You rejected it."

Madeleine took a risk in refusing to change the book. Her publisher took a risk in publishing such an unusual story. By daring failure, both of them reaped enormous rewards.

The Idea in Action

Cindy spent the last 5 years working as a floral designer at a flower shop in a small town. She loved the work, and her designs were really lovely. But after a few years, she began to get restless. Designing was fun, but she had lots of innovative ideas about designs that the shop owner wasn't willing to try. She began to dream about owning her own place.

Cindy knew there was a big difference between the security of working for someone else and the risks of striking out on her own, but the idea continued to tempt her. One day she heard about a small shop for sale in a rural town in the next county. She used every penny of her savings for the down payment, and promised the owner the rest of the money in a balloon payment in 5 years.

For the first 3 years Cindy worried that she had made a mistake. There was a big difference between being an artistic arranger and a hardheaded businesswoman. Some of the dramatic ideas she tried just didn't work in a small, conservative community. The business side of the shop was foreign to her. Hiring and firing employees was a nightmare. The business required long hours and endless nights of worry and planning. Many times she agonized that she should never have taken such a risk.

As she struggled through the first half of her fourth year, however, her outlook began to change. She had gradually learned which ideas weren't practical, and she had abandoned some of her plans. Several small companies moved in, and Cindy began an aggressive campaign to garner more of their business. With each canny new move, her business strengthened. What had looked like a desperate mistake the first year or two was finally turning into a profitable business. By the fifth year, when her balloon payment was due, Cindy had saved enough money to pay off her loan and turn the corner on her new venture. She had gambled everything on herself, and she had won.

For Reflection

Do you have a secret dream that you've been afraid to act on?

Think of what you'll be doing in 5 years if you don't take the risk. Now think how your future could be different if you did. Is it worth it?

Compare the lives of some risk takers you know with those of more conservative people. How are their lives different?

LOOK THE PART

Dress for the position that you want to have—not the one you already have achieved.

In More Depth

It's important to look, act, and dress the part you want to play in your career. If you want to be taken seriously, you've got to look like you're willing to play the game. While the adage "You can't judge a book by its cover" may seem reassuring, in the working world people are judging you by your cover every day. It may not be fair, but it's the way things are. If you arrive for work with torn or dirty clothes, disheveled hair, and a ring in your nose, you are sending a statement just as surely as if you were wearing a sandwich board.

If you doubt this, just look inside any courtroom. You'll never see a lawyer—male or female—dressed inappropriately. They know that appearance counts for a great deal, not just to the judge but especially to the jury. This is why lawyers also counsel their clients on appropriate clothing in the courtroom.

This means business clothing—no exaggerated attire, no evening clothes, no jeans. Be clean, neat, and freshly groomed, and practice good posture. Watch your speaking voice and modulate your tone. Keep your shoes clean, and make sure you have an extra pair of stockings in your purse in case of runs.

The Idea in Action

Connie was hired as an administrative assistant of a large nonprofit professional organization in a metropolitan city. Always somewhat of a free spirit, she managed to wear a conservative skirt and sweater for her interview, but once hired she became more careless about her appearance.

She was bright and creative, and was on track to move up in the organization. But Connie was not always very organized in the morning. She often forgot to sew on buttons or fix rips in her clothing. She never seemed to have time to polish her shoes, and her stockings always seemed to have snags and runs.

No one ever confronted her about her appearance, but a year later Connie noticed that two other assistants in other departments who had been hired about the same time had already been given promotions. Connie knew her own ideas were far more creative, so she confronted her boss. Why wasn't her career going anywhere? "You're bright and talented," her boss told her. "But you don't seem as if you're quite ready for a spot in management. Managers have got to *look* capable and pulled together. You've got to deal with professionals, and you can't look sloppy when you do."

Connie realized the other two assistants always dressed in neat, fashionable suits, low pumps, and a few pieces of understated jewelry. She began putting out her clothing the night before, so she could have time to repair any torn items and make sure everything was pressed. With a new hairstyle and more pulled-together style, she was not surprised when she was promoted within 3 months of her "makeover." It was the best advice she'd ever gotten.

For Reflection

What did you wear to work yesterday? Were there any rips, missing buttons, snags, or dirt smears?

How would your boss rate your work attire?

What are some ways you can guide your employees to understand the need for a good appearance?

The Day to Day

GO THE EXTRA MILE

Without being a martyr, you'll find that it's the little things that really endear you to your employer.

In More Depth

Organizing a messy area, coming up with a way to make a task easier, even showing a genuine interest in the growth or success of the company makes you a valuable asset. All too often, bosses feel that their employees are at work only for the paycheck. It shows. The boss thinks: "If I see one person who really cares, I will go overboard to make her feel valued and appreciated."

In a time when so many people seem to have lost the urge to put themselves out and achieve the highest effort, a person with character and integrity—someone who can be counted on in a pinch—becomes truly invaluable.

The Idea in Action

Jane managed a local boarding kennel while studying for her MBA. She enjoyed the part-time responsibility and working in the open air. She was responsible for grooming many of the animals, exercising the dogs, cleaning their cages, feeding and watering them, and giving medication.

In a business rife with transitory employees, it wasn't long before the owner noticed that Jane never missed a day of work, never called in sick, and never left early. Soon she was given responsibility for ordering feed and picking up supplies. This was followed by a substantial raise. On her own, she outlined a number of potential fire hazards that the busy owner had overlooked. She organized the owner's training schedule and came up with an innovative plan for tracking medication. Although when she was hired the owner in no way had anticipated creating a partnership for the business, within a year Jane had been promoted to partner, with another substantial increase in salary. It was Jane's consistent interest and concern in the business that had sparked the offer. "You have never let me down," the owner told her, "not once in all this time. I can leave the country and not have to worry about the kennel." For that peace of mind, the owner had been willing to reward Jane monetarily and psychologically.

For Reflection

Have you ever "gone the extra mile" for your employer without wondering whether you would be compensated?

Name three things that you could do right now that would show an interest in your job.

Imagine you owned your company. Would you do your job any differently?

JUST DO IT!

Don't get discouraged by those who look at your gender first and your work second. Take advantage of every opportunity that comes along, no matter why it's given to you.

In More Depth

Many women feel that they are always evaluated first as a woman and second a person with certain talents and abilities. This could be quite true, but whether it's true or not doesn't change what you need to do about it. That is—take action. Aristotle understood this when he advised his students that "what we have learned to do, we learn by doing."

Aristotle knew that nobody ever progressed by sitting around complaining about things. Get out there, set a goal, and go for it. If someone is discounting your ability because you're a woman, just keep going. You can prove that person wrong, but only by taking action.

The Idea in Action

When Janet was hired as a new reporter at a small, rural daily paper, she was shocked when she noticed the initial looks she got from the mostly male reporters on her first day. Those looks told her that their opinion about her had already been formed, and nothing she could do or say after that initial observation would make a bit of difference. They assumed she had been hired as a "token" woman. Privately, Janet suspected they might be right.

Later that week, when a call came in to cover a car wreck, the editor passed her over because "we don't like to send women to cover those things." Janet insisted that as the new reporter, it was her turn. It would be unfair to exempt her from an unpleasant duty simply because she was a woman, she argued. Eventually her persistence won her the assignment—and the growing respect of her male colleagues.

Janet knew that she had been given the job in part because she was a woman, but she took the job to prove that her gender was irrelevant to the work at hand. Was it fair that she had to "prove" her worth? No. But refusing this challenge wouldn't do her career any good, and would never teach the others that women could do the job. She also hoped that her own pioneering efforts might make it easier for the generation of women who followed in her footsteps.

For Reflection

Have you ever suspected that you got a job because you were a woman?

Have you ever suspected that others felt you couldn't do the job because you were a woman?

What can you do or say to change these attitudes?

ACCEPT NEW TASKS WILLINGLY

You grow by tackling new jobs you don't already know how to do. It's not always comfortable. But it works.

In More Depth

If it's scary, odds are it's good for you. Take that extra assignment or that promotion that seems like a stretch, and you'll be surprised how quickly you grow to fit the new responsibilities. If you're feeling comfortable in a job—you can do it with your eyes closed—that's a sign you've mastered everything there is to know. It's time to move on.

Of course, moving on and accepting new challenges implies risk. There's always some risk inherent in growing. (Otherwise, *everyone* would do it!) But it's better to take a risk and make a mistake than to be paralyzed by fear and do nothing. Remember, doing *something* is better than doing *nothing* in most cases. Inaction never got anyone anywhere. It is life's difficulties that offers us the best chance to grow. Before you say no to the next challenge, consider what gift it has to offer you.

The Idea in Action

Ginger had been successfully selling magazine articles for years, and recently she had begun branching out, writing her first health book. It was selling moderately well in the bookstores, but she knew that if it was going to do really well the book needed to be promoted. When her publisher called and asked her if she'd be willing to be interviewed on the radio, she panicked. A quiet person who disliked the limelight, Ginger's first impulse was to slam the phone down and hide under her comforter.

Wisely, Ginger realized that if she was going to succeed, she would need to promote herself not just in radio interviews but on TV as well. She agreed to a series of radio interviews that she could do from her home. Before the first interview, she taped up notes for herself all over the kitchen so that she could refer to them in case she froze in fear. By the third interview, she was relaxed enough to joke with the interviewer, and by the fourth she knew she was ready for more challenging interviews. She accepted speaking assignments at local libraries and bookstores, and agreed to her first TV interview. Again, she started small—her hometown TV stations—before branching out at larger regional broadcasters. "Each time I tried a new interview situation, I was terrified. But I learned that each time I finished one interview, the next one would get easier."

For Reflection

How many times in the last month have you been bored on the job?

What new job-related task frightens you the most? That's what you need to work on.

Make a list of challenges you've overcome. Think about what new challenges await you.

LEARN THE LANGUAGE

Men really do perceive things differently from women. To best communicate with men in the workplace, you must understand those differences and use them to your advantage.

In More Depth

Women believe the way to achieve is to build consensus and connections; men believe achievement is built on dominance and verbal performance. The two wildly disparate styles are bound to collide in the workplace if they are not understood.

To many men in business, there is a hierarchy to all human relations—either you're one up or you're one down. For this reason, men tend to jockey for position in a conversation as a way to achieve dominance; they aren't really looking to *connect.* This dominance can be attained by exhibiting knowledge and skill, and by holding "center stage" in the conversation. Early on, men learn they can earn status by giving orders and getting people to follow them.

Many women, on the other hand, have been taught the behavioral opposite to overt aggression and confrontation: We learn to negotiate and be cooperative. Concerned with our place amidst a network of connections, most women seek to build rapport as a way of negotiating relationships.

Neither communication approach is fundamentally right or wrong, but the differences can cause problems for women when the two styles clash. Women who believe that the politics of connection is a positive trait will be misjudged by a man who believes that this style of relating reveals a lack of independence and insecurity. By choosing to express ideas in a mild way so as not to offend, women can appear to male colleagues as uniformed or not assertive enough. In a conversation, a woman's efforts to emphasize similarities and avoid showing off can be interpreted by a man as incompetence or insecurity.

If you find yourself working in a "man's world," read up on books that discuss how men and women communicate in business to gain insight into how each interact in the workplace. Remember that in any interaction, men tend to ask themselves: "Have I won? Do you respect me?" whereas women tend to wonder: "Have I been helpful enough? Do you like me?"

The Idea in Action

Wanda was a marketing director for a large toy company. When she led a project meeting, she would present her plans for a product introduction and, because this was her area of expertise, she would expect agreement and positive response to her plans. Instead, the men on the team, who had no marketing responsibility, would challenge her plans and force her to defend her position. She was frustrated that they could not just accept her decisions and applaud her exciting plans. She felt as though they didn't respect her marketing decisions and that they questioned her judgment.

When Wanda brought up the problem to her mentor, an older woman experienced in business, the woman advised that she read several books on male-female communication styles. What Wanda read astonished her. She finally understood that men commonly challenged authority of others in order to maintain status and position within a group. However, most women misinterpret this challenge as a personal attack on their credibility.

Once Wanda understood that the men in her group were not attacking her personally, she was able to stop responding defensively to what she perceived as an attack but was, in fact, a communication style.

For Reflection

When you are speaking in front of a group, how do you present yourself?

Do you find it easier to seek consensus or simply assert your own position?

What would happen if you changed your style?

TRY TO HAVE AN ADVENTURE EVERY DAY

You don't have to make a daily bungee jump. But put in the effort to make something special out of every day.

In More Depth

German writer Rainer Maria Rilke noted that it's possible to make something special of your life, no matter how humdrum it may seem to everyone else. "If your life seems poor, don't blame it; blame yourself," Rilke wrote. "Tell yourself that you are not poet enough to call forth its riches. For to the creator, there is no poverty and no poor, indifferent place."

Rilke probably wasn't juggling family, relationships, home, and/or work when he wrote those lines. What he understood is that joy takes effort—not money. You may not be able to jump on a plane to the Canary Islands when things get tough. Having an adventure every day is really about how you *look* at life, what approach you take to handling your responsibilities. With the wrong attitude, almost any job can become a chore. By consciously deciding to change the way you approach your life *just for today*, you'll be amazed at how more upbeat you feel.

When she was a young mother of three, Newbery Award winner Madeleine L'Engle remembers how hard it was to manage her three children, run the family's country store, and write in between. No matter how hectic her life, however, there were always candles on her dinner table. The family might have been eating only chili or stew, but they ate it by candlelight. Somehow, she says, it made a difference.

Somehow, it was magical.

The Idea in Action

Hilary was the mother of four children under age 6. She had given up her job as secretary to stay at home with her babies, and most of the time she was glad she did, although money was tight. But the stress of keeping up with the children and running the house, and the lack of adult conversation and interaction during the day, was taking its toll.

Two of her youngsters were still in diapers the day the washer broke. Hilary was already late for the third child's half-day preschool, a situation which was made worse when she realized the car's gas tank was almost empty. The gas station was on the way to school, but she was short of cash and the bank machine was in the opposite direction. As she was sitting in traffic praying the car would get by on gas fumes, the fourth child—who had been cranky all morning—spilled a bottle of juice all over the back seat. It was all too much. No one should be expected to be able to cope with four babies, she thought. Just then she happened to glance across the street. On a bench in the park was an old woman, sitting alone and sprinkling crumbs to a flock of pigeons at her feet. Behind her a carousel was just starting its ride.

To the children's utter astonishment, Hilary abruptly drove into the park and led them all over to the ride. As she watched them whirling round and round, laughing with delight, preschool forgotten, the tensions of the morning evaporated.

"When I saw the old woman all alone on that bench, I realized how precious this time with my children was," Hilary recalls. "Sure they drive me crazy. But before long, they'll all be gone. I might be that woman on the bench, all alone. If that happens, I don't want to remember the broken washers and the spilled juice. I want to remember the carousels."

For Reflection

Do your days stretch out before you in a series of bleak, unexciting moments?

When was the last time you left your responsibilities to do something impetuous, just for you?

At the end of the day, can you think of one silly thing you did just because it made you—or someone else—happy?

MAKE SURE YOU HAVE A SUPPORT SYSTEM

You need support at work—people with whom you can discuss career problems. You need support at home—people with whom you can talk about the kids, your spouse, your family, your relationships. You need friends to nourish your spirit.

In More Depth

You need a personal support system. Countless research studies consistently reach the same conclusions: The people who survive the longest are those who have established some type of support system. Ideally, this support system includes a live-in "significant other," but it shouldn't be limited to the person with whom you're living. (After all, "others" can cause stress on their own!) And certainly, if you're in an *unhappy* situation at home, this may cause more stress than it alleviates.

But loving bonds with friends, family, and community can make a real difference in the quality—and quantity—of your life. If at some point you find you don't *have* a support system, you need to find one—meet new people, reestablish old friendships—or buy one, if you have to, by going into therapy. Just make sure that there is at least one person besides yourself to whom you can seek counsel.

Support systems at work can give your career a jump start. In your job, you may have to make unpopular decisions. You may feel as if you're in the middle of a group of conflicting voices, all trying to win you to their point of view. You need to be able to consult with at least one person in your support system who has an understanding of management and leadership, who can provide balance to your career stress.

It's also a good idea to build a solid support system of people who don't work with you, so you can let off steam about work without fear that someone will squeal to the boss about your true feelings.

On the home front, personal support systems can provide balance and a respite as you struggle with issues of power and conciliation that typify all human relationships.

The Idea in Action

Cheryl had worked for the past 5 years as a writer for a nonprofit association in Boston. When she was promoted to managing editor, her role changed abruptly and she felt isolated and upset. The new position brought with it a range of new in-house political issues that she had never before confronted. As editor, she was placed in the position of evaluating her former peers' work, which she found difficult and which she felt they resented. She was dealing with enormous pressure to put out larger and larger newspapers with fewer and fewer employees.

In the past, she would have gone out to lunch with the other writers to grouse about the problems—something she realized was no longer appropriate. She was no longer invited along on lunch dates with them, and at parties she felt the gulf between them widen inexorably.

One day, at a publishers' convention Cheryl met another editor at a similar nonprofit association with offices down the street. This woman had also recently been promoted, and the two shared coffee after the meeting. They had such a good time talking about their respective on-the-job problems that they vowed to have lunch together every Friday. Cheryl found herself looking forward to these meetings and was far better able to cope with the everyday frustrations, now that she had a colleague on her level.

For Reflection

How many people can you list as part of your support system?
What steps can you take right now to enlarge your support system?

The Big Picture

LIFE ISN'T FAIR

Life isn't always fair. In fact, unpleasant things do happen to very good people, and they happen all the time. The measure of character lies in how you deal with that unfairness.

In More Depth

You can play by all the rules in the book, but chances are that someday you're going to run head on into disappointment. Odds are, you won't have done anything wrong to invite this problem. Maybe your company is downsizing, and your job is on the "eliminate" list. Maybe you have a personality clash with your boss and realize you'll have to find another job. Maybe another woman has sabotaged your career.

Sometimes it seems as if the world was just meant to break your heart. In fact, it's really nothing nearly so personal. Bad things *do* happen to good people. How you cope with the rough spots will, in part, affect how you are able to deal with difficulty in the future.

The Idea in Action

Anne was an extremely successful manager who had been asked to analyze the effectiveness of three departments in her midsize medical equipment company. Because she was a good corporate player who believed in doing what was right for the company, she pointed out ways in which the current organization was not effective. Part of her conclusions included suggestions for a restructuring of the organization which put her own job in jeopardy.

Anne really believed that because she was a valued employee who was doing the right thing, even if her job was eliminated her bosses would find another spot for her. She reasoned that she was the kind of employee the company would want to keep.

Anne *was* an excellent employee, and the company thought her restructuring proposal made sense. They promptly initiated the restructuring, eliminated her job, and laid her off. "I remember verbalizing that I was doing the right thing, the corporate thing," Anne recalls. "I was doing what was right. It was shocking to see that it was rewarded in a layoff."

While the layoff clearly wasn't fair, Anne recognized that there was no point in grumbling about it. Bitterness wouldn't find her another job. Instead of feeling sorry for herself, she got to work setting up her own consulting firm. These contacts led her to a far better position as a top executive for another company.

Anne hasn't decided never to give an honest evaluation again, but she has made up her mind that in a similar situation, she would line up other options before putting her own job at risk. "I believe you need to do the right, just, fair thing," she says now. "But you have to do it with sanity."

For Reflection

When life deals you an unfair hand, how do you react?

Do your reactions to unfairness imply that life does *"owe" you something?*

Think about how you will react the next time you are confronted with unfairness. Can you consciously choose a different response?

YOU'RE NOT THE CENTER OF THE UNIVERSE

Don't assume that everything that happens is your fault. The world is not usually so black and white.

In More Depth

The more unsure of yourself you are, the more likely you are to judge everything from an egocentric position, placing yourself in the center of every situation. In this sense, being egocentric doesn't mean that you see yourself as superior to everyone else—it's just that you see everyone else's reactions as the direct result of something you've done or said.

Women who see themselves as the cause of every problem, as the instigator of every communication breakdown, often spend a great deal of time trying to figure out exactly how the land lies. They are sometimes referred to as "hypervigilant," constantly scanning their world to prepare for the next catastrophe, which they believe is looming on the horizon.

The Idea in Action

Christine was an account manager in a large brokerage firm. One day her boss stormed into the office and snapped at a comment Christine had made about a current project. Christine retreated to her office in an agony of concern, closing the door and trying to puzzle out what she had done to make her boss so angry. Was he unhappy with her client list? Did he think she wasn't pulling her weight? She spent the entire morning fretting over what she might have done or said to have angered her boss. Then, as she walked by his office on her way to lunch, she heard him on the phone apologizing to his wife for an argument they had had that morning.

"Suddenly, I realized that his bad mood had nothing to do with me," Christine recalled. "He had snapped at me simply because he'd had an argument with his wife that morning."

Over lunch, she confessed her reaction to two co-workers. Both women confessed that they had also assumed *they* had somehow made the boss angry, and that they too had spent the morning trying to figure out what they had done to spark his ire.

For Reflection

Do you automatically assume that other people's reactions are your direct responsibility?

How many times in the last month have you worried about the source of a co-worker's anger?

The next time something goes wrong at work, try to step back from the situation and analyze what the problem might be.

DO WHAT YOU LOVE AND LOVE WHAT YOU DO

The work that you accomplish is part of the story of your life. You get only one life and one story, so choose work that you love, that you're good at, and that matters to you as more than the source of financial security.

In More Depth

When you find a job you really love, convince the people to hire you. Bug them until they do. "Unfortunately, I had many jobs that weren't a good fit because I didn't think about what a good match would be," says one woman entrepreneur. "Since I never did find a great match, I created my own business."

Not everyone has the luxury to do this; sometimes *any* job is better than no job. Of course, security does have a role in your decision making, but whenever possible, you shouldn't choose a job primarily because you think it will deliver security. Security won't pull you through the times when the job is boring or difficult or stressful or overwhelming, but a love of the work *will*.

Follow your heart and do what you want to do. Above all, don't worry about what anyone else says about your goals. "The important thing is to find something you enjoy doing and get paid for it," says Ellen, a North Carolina weaver. "I don't think I could stand to work in an office. That's just not me."

The Idea in Action

Six years ago, Suzy decided she was tired of working in a design firm. She wanted to go out on her own and set up her own studio—but that first step was almost impossible for her to take. She was worried that everyone would see her choice as a step down, that choosing to work at home was not really a career choice. She was afraid that people weren't going to respect her. After agonizing over her move for several months, she finally decided that she would do what *she* wanted to do.

What she discovered was that her friends, co-workers, and family were all delighted with her choice and her courage in striking out on her own. She believes that the fears that were holding her back were really just in her own mind and were not an accurate reflection of what others thought. As a way of boosting her own self-image as an owner of a crafts studio, she networks extensively and subscribes to professional magazines and crafts reports. She has discovered that public respect for the job seems to be a problem for many crafters, who believe that others dismiss their work as something less than "true" art, delegating crafts to the arena of campers, children, and hospital patients.

For Reflection

Do you find yourself dreaming about doing something other than your current job?

What would it take to start living your dream?

Envision your dream job 5 years from now. Make a list of 10 things you can do today to get yourself moving in that direction.

YOU CAN CHANGE YOUR MIND

Be prepared to change your mind about what you love doing. No matter what job you have chosen, it's okay to change horses in midstream.

In More Depth

You may be fortunate enough to discover the work that fulfills you most from the very beginning of your working life. But as complex and multitalented as you are, don't be surprised if part way down your career path, you discover a fork in the road that intrigues you! If you think it might lead to something else you would love doing, you owe it to yourself to consider changing course.

The Idea in Action

Sandra got her degree in English and found a job she loved as an account representative for a midsize advertising agency. She liked her co-workers, the freedom and the responsibility of her position, and the creative potential.

After a number of years, her life had taken a very different path from her early experience when she first joined the agency. She got divorced, remarried, and adopted a newborn child. As her home life radically changed, the work life no longer seemed like a good fit. She became restless and recalled her original dream of teaching. She was also unhappy about spending so much time away from her daughter, and worried about who would care for the child in the summers when she reached school age. As a high school English teacher, Sandra reasoned, she would be at home on vacations and summers with her daughter.

Recognizing these important considerations and allowing herself the freedom to change careers, she is now halfway through a master's program in education that will give her an advanced degree and teaching certification by the time her daughter is ready for school.

For Reflection

Are you as happy with your career as you were when you first started your job?

If there were no obstacles in your way, what job would you like to have?

How would your life change if you switched careers?

DON'T TAKE LIFE TOO SERIOUSLY

"All of life's pieces were in my pocket. One day, I would be a better hand at the game. One day I would learn how to laugh."
—*Herman Hesse*

In More Depth

There is no security in any job for any person. So work hard, keep your options open, and never forget how to laugh. Even if your working situation is unpleasant, there is only so much you can do to change it. This doesn't mean that you should go through life not caring about anything, but you don't have to blow up every problem out of all proportion, either. Ask yourself whether the problem will matter 10 or 20 years from now.

And remember, not for nothing does the word *vacation* derive from the Latin *vacatio*—to be empty and free. If you find yourself getting far too serious about everything in your life, it's time to schedule a *vacatio*. A few days in a new environment should help give you a new perspective.

The Idea in Action

Ellen is the owner of a professional stable whose primary clients are the adolescent daughters of her town's wealthiest parents. A former Grand Prix jumper, Ellen boards expensive show ponies and trains the girls to compete in the jumping ring.

In the past, she drove her students relentlessly, pushing each one to compete on the "A" circuit. She regularly lost her temper, shouting and screaming at the girls when they failed to perform or made mistakes in the stable. Divorced shortly after she opened her stable, Ellen felt driven to succeed as a direct result of her husband's abandonment.

As the pressure mounted, her temper became shorter and began to interfere with her business. Some parents became concerned at her manner, and pulled their daughters from the program. Finally, one of Ellen's best friends had a long talk with her. "When was the last time you got on a horse, just for fun?" her friend asked her. "When was the last time you laughed?" Ellen was shocked into realizing she had stopped enjoying life.

Today, she rarely takes her students to the top-rated shows. Much of her time is spent at smaller meets and local shows, where the children can enjoy themselves without having to compete for points in a cutthroat race to be the best. She looks back on those frenetic days and shakes her head.

"I took it all too seriously," she says today. "I thought I had to be the best. I didn't realize that there was more to the world than winning at all costs. Now I'm enjoying myself, and I love what I'm doing again."

For Reflection

When was the last time you had a good laugh?

If you have trouble putting things in perspective, pretend that tomorrow is your last day on earth. Do your problems pale in comparison?

Think back over the past year. How many times did stress overwhelm you? Did all that stress make your life any better?

DON'T GET DEVOURED

Don't let your job eat you up. Although starting a new business might require a big investment of time up front, if you find yourself continuing to spend every waking moment on the job, including nights, weekends, and holidays, you are at risk of being devoured by your work.

In More Depth

Almost everyone has times when the job seems to take on a life of its own. Rush orders, unexpected emergencies, and important projects can—and should—command a bit of extra effort. But if you find that you invest every single moment of your life on the job and that you don't really enjoy what you're doing any more, it's time to take stock.

How long has this workaholic marathon been going on? Are you truly expected to invest so much of yourself, or have you been pushing yourself because of your own needs or beliefs?

If you own your own business, maybe it's about time to hand some of the lesser responsibilities over to someone else so that you can take more time for yourself. Since people tend to live up to the standards expected of them, you may be pleasantly surprised at the response when you give your employees more responsibility. You'll find delegation benefits both of you, with more autonomy on their part and more relaxation time on yours.

The Idea in Action

Linda has owned and operated a massage center for the past 15 years. Today, she has six independent contractors working for her as well as three part-time support staffers. It has been an enormous effort to nurture the business from the beginning to its present size. At times, the effort totally took over her life.

Over the years, Linda had missed birthday parties, anniversaries, vacations, school presentations, and even funerals because she felt she had to "be there " for her business. And yet the more time she spent in the business, the less satisfied she became.

Today, she has developed the attitude that "it will all work out" and that people will make do. "Whatever comes up, I just deal with it," she says matter of factly. "So we lose $100. It's not the end of the world." She no longer kills herself in order to keep the business running perfectly—and now it's thriving. She goes in only 2 days a week, and yet the business supports her with a good income. The people who work there love it and take excellent care of the business when she's not around. "I just wish it hadn't taken me so long to adopt this more relaxed attitude," she reports.

For Reflection

How many weeks have you logged in more than 40 hours? More than 60 hours?

What would happen if you started delegating tasks to your employees?

Have you ever missed important engagements because you just couldn't take time off from work?

CREATE YOUR OWN DESTINY

Nobody owes you anything, so don't waste time complaining. Craft your life so that it fits only you.

In More Depth

The idea of entitlement—that the world really does owe you a living—can be found in both men and women. The seeds of these feelings are usually sown in childhood, when every whim has been granted and every wish fulfilled. Upon reaching adulthood, these spoiled individuals expect that life will continue to shower them with riches.

In fact, there is no such thing as a free lunch, and even the snacks between meals carry a price. That being the case, there's no point in complaining when the world doesn't go your way. Most times, it won't.

The real test of your character is what you choose to do when life gets difficult. Do you kick the cat and complain about the unfairness, or do you quit grousing and get moving?

The Idea in Action

Laurie earned a master's degree in electrical engineering and held down a rewarding job at a major communications company in the Northeast. She was on a managerial track at the company when her first daughter, Rachel, was born.

Up to that point, she thought her career was all she ever wanted, and she never envisioned wanting to leave the path she had marked out for herself. All this changed once she gave birth to her daughter. But she found the decision to leave the company was agonizing, primarily because she knew her superiors expected that she would stay. She felt as if she were "selling out" her sex by abandoning a high-status career that would have been unavailable to most women a few generations earlier. She also felt that her choice would be criticized by her professional, unmarried friends.

As she suspected, her superiors were stunned when Laurie decided to leave the company. The pressure of their expectations—and the implicit disapproval—was particularly difficult to handle. Still, Laurie decided that being able to stay at home with her children—carving out her own destiny—was more important than caving in to her boss's expectations.

Shortly after leaving the firm, she set up her own software company and today is busy raising her family while running a successful business at home. "I feel I'm doing something important for my children," she says. "I'm giving them the start that they need in life to succeed and fulfill their own dreams."

For Reflection

Are you able to accept setbacks as a normal part of life and work?

Can you let go of your anger when things don't go your way, and plot your next move?

Remember the last time things didn't go the way you planned. How did you handle it? Could you have done something differently?

ALWAYS OPERATE FROM A POSITION OF STRENGTH

Take time to think about every situation in which you find yourself before you must act. Don't go blindly into any situation, hoping for the best. Never assume that others will take care of you or look out for you.

In More Depth

Anyone who has ever watched a superb trial attorney in action has seen how effective it can be to operate from a position of strength. No matter what objections pop up from the prosecutor, no matter how angrily the judge demands information, the superior trial attorney seems to effortlessly jab and parry, never losing her cool.

If only it was as easy to do this in real life! The truth of the matter is that all too often, we lose our tempers. We get flustered, we flounder, we resort to an attack with thoughtless remarks instead of studied responses.

All too often, many women—whether it is an inborn trait or whether they have been socialized to behave this way—become emotional under stress.

When you operate from a position of strength, you are unflappable. You are cool, you are resolute. You cannot be goaded. By marshaling your wits and refusing to be drawn into an emotional argument, you can increase the odds of staying on top of a situation. Whether you are arguing with your spouse over a household matter or battling your boss for a raise, operating from a position of strength will give you power.

The Idea in Action

Sarah wanted a raise. She *needed* a raise. She worked harder than anyone else in her division, and her ideas were solid and successful. Expenses at home were increasing and she was worried about meeting her mortgage obligations. As a single mom responsible for a young son, she had learned she couldn't count on child support checks arriving on time. She just *had* to have more money.

She'd been stewing over her situation for several weeks. One day, she went in to her boss and blurted, "I need a raise. It's been more than a year since my last raise, and I think I'm due." At the sight of her boss's face, she faltered. "Things are really tight at home, financially. I just…" She broke off as she felt her face flush bright red.

Her supervisor raised her eyes and snapped, "Well, it's not a good time right now. I'm being pressured to cut back, and I can't go to the president with salary requests right now. Maybe later in the year." Crushed, Sarah crept back to her office. "That's not the way you ask for a raise," advised her officemate when Sarah had related the conversation. "You have to prove to them why you *deserve* a raise. You can't just tell them you *need* one."

This approach made sense. For the next week, Sarah researched her past job performance. On Friday, she set up an appointment with her boss and presented her findings. She discussed how the implementation of her brochure campaign had brought in significant revenue; she charted the exact figures on a graph. Her ideas about desktop publishing for the new catalog had logged another impressive $125,000 savings. By adding up all her extra responsibilities and hours she had willingly undertaken, Sarah was able to show *in dollars and cents* that she was an extremely valuable employee who had consistently increased both her responsibilities and her company's income. The

bottom line, she concluded, was that she was responsible for a significant increase in the company's income and therefore deserved a raise.
Her boss agreed, and was so impressed with Sarah's presentation that
she was also given a promotion and a bigger office.

For Reflection

Have you ever been caught off guard and left floundering for a response?

What method do you use to "stay cool" in a tense situation so you can review your options?

What first step could you take toward developing a new emphasis of operating from a position of strength?

About the Author

Carol A. Turkington has written eleven books, in addition to this one. She is also a frequent contributor to *Self*, *Vogue*, *The New York Times* syndicate, and many other publications.